NORTH AMERICAN DINOSAURS

ALLOSAURUS

Darlene Stille

Rourke
Publishing LLC
Vero Beach, Florida 32964

About The Author

Darlene Stille is a science writer and an author of more than 80 books for young people. When she was in high school she fell in love with science. While attending the University of Illinois, she discovered that she also loved writing. She was fortunate to find a career as an editor and writer that allowed her to combine both her interests. Darlene Stille now lives and writes in Michigan.

www.rourkepublishing.com

Photos/Illustrations: Cover and page 14 © Joe Tucciarone; title page © Luis Rey; page 4 © Michael Carroll; page 6 © Chris Butler, Photo Researchers; pages 8, 12 18, 19 © American Museum of Natural History Library; page 10 © Gerhard Boeggemann; page 16 © Christian Darkin, Photo Researchers; page 20 © Jan Sovak; page 22 © Francois Gohier

Editor: Robert Stengard-Olliges

Cover and page design by Nicola Stratford

Library of Congress Cataloging-in-Publication Data

Stille, Darlene R.
 Allosaurus / by Darlene Stille.
   p. cm. -- (North American dinosaurs)
 ISBN 1-60044-250-1
 1. Allosaurus--Juvenile literature. 2. Dinosaurs--North America--Juvenile literature. I. Title. II. Series.
 QE862.S3S75 2007
 567.912--dc22
                              2006016094
Printed in the USA

CG/CG

Rourke Publishing

www.rourkepublishing.com – sales@rourkepublishing.com
Post Office Box 3328, Vero Beach, FL 32964

Table of Contents

Mighty Hunters

Gigantic jaws fly open. Sharp teeth flash in the sun. A pack of dinosaurs leaps out from behind a pile of rocks. The dinosaurs are *allosaurs*–hungry *allosaurs*!

They have spotted their dinner. Dinner is a big plant-eating dinosaur munching on **ferns** beside a river. Its long tail swings back and forth. Too late, the plant-eater spies the *allosaurs*. The plant-eater tries to run away, but it cannot run fast enough. The plant-eater is no match for the *allosaurs*.

Allosaurs were mighty hunters. They probably hunted in packs of two or more. They were carnivores. They only ate meat, which means they often ate other dinosaurs.

Allosaur's *big jaws and sharp teeth made it a mighty hunter.*

A Chunky Dinosaur

Allosaur had a thick body that ended in a long tail. An *allosaur* was as long as a freight train **boxcar**. Some *allosaurs* weighed as much as a small truck. Big bones and strong muscles made *allosaurs* powerful, too.

Allosaur *walked on its hind legs and had large, bony ridges over each eye.*

Allosaur looked very frightening. It could rear up and walk on its chunky back legs. It was almost as tall as a two-story house. Allosaur could have looked into an upstairs window!

Skull bones help scientists figure out what allosaur's head looked like. An allosaur skull was as long as a yardstick. Bony bumps stuck up over each eye. The bumps made ridges that looked like eyebrows. Looking at skull bones helps artists draw the face of an allosaur.

The Better to Eat With

Rip! *Allosaur* teeth tear into its prey. The teeth had a jagged edge like a saw. These teeth were made for eating meat.

Allosaur teeth were two to four inches (five to 10 cm) long. They curved backward. The curved teeth grabbed and held onto meat.

The teeth were set in big **jaws**. Like a snake, *allosaur* could open its jaws very wide. The jaws gobbled up big chunks of meat. *Allosaur* could bite off 100 pounds (45 kg) of meat at a time! It could eat an animal as big as a police dog in one bite.

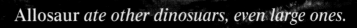
Allosaur *ate other dinosuars, even large ones.*

Claws!

Allosaur had long legs in back and short arms in front. These arms were too short to use for walking, but they did have claws. *Allosaur* used its sharp claws to help catch dinner.

Each arm ended in three fingers. Each finger ended in a long, sharp claw. The claws were as long as a ruler and curved like hooks. *Allosaur* clutched meat with these claws and ate by tearing off bites with their big teeth and jaws.

Allosaur *used its short front arms to hold while using its strong jaws to tear off bites to eat.*

Fiercest Jurassic Dinosaurs

Allosaur lived near water where it could catch and eat other dinosaurs.

Allosaur roamed Earth a long time ago. It lived from about 206 million to 144 million years ago. This time was called the **Jurassic** Period. The land where *allosaur* lived is now the American West.

Allosaur was the fiercest of all the Jurassic dinosaurs. There were more *allosaurs* than any other kind of dinosaur.

Allosaur stomped over rocks and sand on its powerful back legs. It used its keen eyes to search the hot, dry land. *Allosaur* hunted along the banks of lakes and rivers. Big plant-eating dinosaurs munched on ferns and the leaves of trees that grew along the banks. They slurped water from the lakes and rivers. *Allosaur* lived where the plant-eaters lived. The plant-eaters were food for *allosaur*.

Allosaur Dinners

Any kind of animal could wind up as an *allosaur's* dinner. Because *allosaur* hunted in groups, it could bring down a dinosaur much bigger than it was.

Sometimes *allosaur* dined on *Diplodocus*. *Diplodocus* was the biggest dinosaur that ever lived on land. It was almost three times

This allosaur *is hunting an apatosaur.*

bigger than most *allosaurs*. *Allosaur* also
hunted *apatosaurs*. An *apatosaur* had a long
neck like a giraffe.

Allosaur even chased big *stegosaurs* with
stiff plates on their backs. The plates were
made of bone and stuck up like spikes. But
even these plates could not keep a *stegosaur*
from becoming an *allosaur* dinner.

A Fast Runner

Allosaur left clues about how it ran. The clues are in *allosaur* tracks. *Allosaur* made the tracks when its big legs and feet squished into soft mud. The mud hardened into stone.

The tracks show that *allosaur* legs ended in feet with four toes. One toe pointed backward. The backward toe helped *allosaur* balance when it ran. Spaces between the tracks show that *allosaurs* could have zipped along at 40 miles per hour.

Footprints that have turned to fossils give scientists clues about how allosaurus moved.

Allosaurs fell a lot when they ran. Skeletons of *allosaurs* show many broken bones. *Allosaurs* fell forward when they ran. Their short arms could not help them. The *allosaurs* broke ribs and other bones, but that did not keep them from chasing other dinosaurs.

Allosaur Babies

Scientists have found fossils of *allosaur* eggs in nests. They know that *allosaurs* hatched from eggs, just like baby chickens do.

An adult *allosaur* probably dug a hole in the ground and made a nest. The female *allosaur* laid more than 100 eggs in the nest. Then she covered up the nest with dirt and guarded the eggs.

The baby *allosaurs* that hatched looked like grown-up *allosaurs*, just smaller. The babies hunted insects and small animals. In just seven years, these babies would be all grown up. They would be ready to have babies of their own.

Allosaurs belonged to a special dinosaur group. The group was called the **theropods**. Some theropods were huge. Other theropods were small.

All theropods ate meat and walked on two legs. They had hips like birds. Theropods may even have had colorful feathers.

Many scientists do not think that all dinosaurs died out. They think that some theropods just changed over time to become the birds of today.

An allosaur *mother guarding her nest.*

Discovering Allosaurs

The first *allosaur* bones came from Colorado. The bones had become fossils, or turned to stone. Fossil hunters dug up many bones in Colorado and Utah. They found that the bones belonged to many kinds of dinosaurs.

Fossil hunters have found many allosaur bones in Colorado and Utah.

One of the bones they found was part of a backbone. This backbone was different from the backbones of other dinosaurs. A scientist named the dinosaur that the backbone came from *Allosaurus*. The name means "different lizard."

Allosaurs slowly disappeared. They became extinct, or died off, about 144 million years ago. Other meat-eating dinosaurs took their place, including **Tyrannosaurus rex**.

Glossary

boxcar (BOKS kar) — freight train car with roof on top and sliding doors on each side

fern (FURN) — plant that has feathery leaves but no flowers

jaw (JAW) — bone that holds teeth and opens and closes the mouth

Jurassic (JOO ras ik) — time on Earth from 208 million to 144 million years ago.

theropod (thir uh pahd) — a meat-eating, two-legged dinosaur with short arms

Tyrannosaurus rex (ti ran uh sor us REKS) — a big, meat-eating dinosaur

Index

Further Reading

Bennett, Leonie. *Dinosaurs That Ate Meat.*
   Bearport Publishing, 2006.

Quigley, Mary. *Dinosaur Digs.* Heinemann, 2005.

Roberts, Russell. *Where Did All the Dinosaurs Go?*
   Mitchell Lane Publishers, 2005.

Websites to Visit

http://yahooligans.yahoo.com/content/science/dinosaurs/dino_card/3
.html

http://www.abc.net.au/dinosaurs/big_al/default.htm

www.cr.nps.gov/museum/exhibits/dino/index.html